The French Revolution, 1789–94

FOUNDATION

JOHN D. CLARE

Hodder Murray

A MEMBER OF THE HODDER HEADLINE GROUP

Acknowledgements

The front cover shows 'The Tennis Court Oath' (1789), by J-L David and a portrait of Maximilien de Robespierre reproduced courtesy of Photothèque des Musées de la Ville de Paris.

The publishers would like to thank the following individuals, institutions and companies for permission to reproduce copyright illustrations in this book:

AKG Photo London pages 9, 17, 20-21, 27, 29 (top), 37 (top), 42 (bottom left and right), 43 (top); Artwork designed by Anet Meyer/Second Harvest Food Bank of Orange County page 15 (bottom); Bibliotheque Nationale de France page 22 (bottom); The British Library pages 37 (bottom), 40 (745A6); The British Museum page 41 (DG 9427); Corbis pages 3 (top right), 6, 19, 22 (top); Phototheque des Musees de la Ville de Paris pages 3 (bottom), 15 (top), 16, 23, 28, 29 (bottom), 33, 34, 35, 38, 39 (top), 42 (top left), 43 (bottom).

The publishers would also like to thank the following for permission to reproduce material in this book:
Definition on page 4 reproduced from the Collins Shorter Contemporary Dictionary, 1972, with kind permission of HarperCollins Publishers; David Higham Associates Limited for the extracts from *The French Revolution* by Christopher Hibbert, Penguin, 1982; Linda Kelly for the extracts from *Women of the French Revolution* by Linda Kelly, Hamish Hamilton, 1987; Extracts from *Citizens: A Chronicle of the French Revolution* by Simon Schama, Viking, 1989, copyright © Simon Schama, 1989, reproduced by permission of Penguin Books Ltd.

Every effort has been made to trace and acknowledge ownership of copyright. The publishers will be glad to make suitable arrangements with any copyright holders whom it has not been possible to contact.

Orders: please contact Bookpoint Ltd, 130 Milton Park, Abingdon, Oxon OX14 4SB. Telephone: (44) 01235 827720, Fax: (44) 01235 400454. Lines are open from 9.00 – 5.00, Monday to Saturday, with a 24 hour message answering service. You can also order through our website at www.hoddereducation.co.uk

British Library Cataloguing in Publication Data
A catalogue record for this title is available from The British Library

ISBN-10: 0 340 78951 4
ISBN-13: 978 0 340 78951 3

First published 2001
Impression number   10 9 8 7 6 5
Year   2006

Copyright © 2001 John D Clare

Typeset by Liz Rowe
Printed in Italy for Hodder Murray, an imprint of Hodder Education, a member of the Hodder Headline Group, 338 Euston Road, London NW1 3BH.

Contents

1 WHAT IS A REVOLUTION?

IN THIS CHAPTER YOU WILL LEARN:
- What a revolution is;
- THREE changes of the French Revolution.

A revolution

A revolution is one whole turn. If a wheel goes round once, it has made one 'revolution'.

Sometimes history, too, seems to turn round
5 and go in a different way.

Historians call these times 'revolutions'.

Q

1. How many things can you think of that go round? Can you think of any things that are measured in rpm – 'revolutions per minute'?

2. Do you know any 'revolutions' in History?

Before 1789, the poor people were not allowed to kill the lords' rabbits or birds.

'Long live the Revolutions!'

The French Revolution

In 1789, there was a big change in the government of France.

1. Before 1789, the king – King 10
Louis XVI – had all the power.
He said that God gave him the right to run the government in the way he wanted. Nobody could say 'No' to the king. 15

2. Before 1789, the rich people had most of the land and money. They had rights that other people did not have. The poor people did all 20
the work for them.

3. Before 1789, the Church in France had lots of land and money.

SOURCE A

▲ *This picture shows the lords being made to give up all their land and money during the Revolution.*

SOURCE C

▲ *A drawing, made after 1793, showing what happened to Louis XVI in the Revolution.*

SOURCE B

After   *Before*

▲ *Before and after! This drawing shows what happened to the priests. In 1792, the poor people killed many priests.*

Tasks

1. Match **Sources A–C** on page 3 against points 1–3 on page 2 (*lines 10–24*).

2. Imagine you are either:

● The king
● A lord
● A priest
● A poor person

Give a short talk to the rest of the class, saying what happened to you in the Revolution, and what you thought about it.

3. Use these ideas to draw a poster, 'The French Revolution: Before and After'.

How unequal was France?

Arthur Young

In 1787, an English man called Arthur Young went to France. He thought that it was a very dirty and poor place.

5   One day, walking up a long hill, he met a poor woman. She looked about 70 years old. She told him that France was a sad country.

'Why?', asked Arthur Young.

The woman told him that she had a small farm,
10   one cow and 7 children – but she had to pay rent to two different lords, as well as taxes to the government. Something had to be done, because the taxes were killing them, she said.

Arthur Young asked her how old she was.
15   She told him that she was 28.

'The poor people are very poor,' he wrote.

Rich and poor

Before 1789, France was a place where the rich had money and rights, but many people had
20   nothing. The table below tells you about the different classes in France.

Look at the table. Was France before 1789 a *fair* place to live?

Who	How Many	Had
King	1 family	He had all the power.
The Church	About 130,000 people.	1/10th of the land. People had to give the Church 1/10th of everything they grew.
The Lords	About 400,000 people.	1/5th of the land. The lords did not pay taxes.
Everybody else	25 million people.	They had to pay all the taxes, but had no say in how the country was run.

One lord made the poor people in his village stay up all night, hitting the frogs, to stop them croaking and keeping him awake!

SOURCE A

Mud houses, no windows. How can the lord live next to people so dirty and poor?

 Arthur Young, writing about a village in France he saw in 1788.

SOURCE B

1. We want the king to stop the taxes on food.

2. We want the lords to pay tax like we do.

3. We should not have to build roads that only the lords will go on.

4. We should be able to kill the rabbits and birds.

Written by the people of the village of Longes in 1789.

WHAT IS A REVOLUTION?

The King and Queen.

The lords had lots of land and money, but did not have to pay taxes.

The Church had lots of land and money, but it did not have to pay taxes.

The King could put anyone he wanted into prison.

The King's Palace at Versailles – good food, good clothes, good fun.

France before 1789.

Poor people paid all the taxes.
Poor people had to work for the lords.

Poor people were very poor. They had no say in how the country was run.

A man who was not alive in the years before 1789 does not know what 'the Good Life' is.

Written by Talleyrand, who was a bishop.

Tasks

1. Why did the poor woman on page 4 look so old, do you think?

2. What did Arthur Young mean in **Source A**?

3. Suggest reasons why the people of Longes wanted each of the 4 things in **Source B**.

4. 'A sad country' or 'the Good Life'. Who do you agree with – the poor woman on page 4 or the bishop on page 5?

2 WHAT CAUSED THE FRENCH REVOLUTION?

IN THIS CHAPTER YOU WILL LEARN:

- **ELEVEN** causes of the French revolution;
- The **THREE** Estates in the Estates-General;
- What really happened on Bastille Day, 1789.

cause, short-term,

prices, harvest

Estates-General: a kind of Parliament of the French people.

ideas, freedom

The long and the short of it

Few things in History have just one cause – most things have many causes. The French Revolution had lots of causes –

5 it takes a lot to make people kill their king!

Some of the causes of the French Revolution went back many, many years. Historians

10 call these the *long-term causes*. Some causes happened in 1789, just before the Revolution; historians call these the *short-term causes*.

❶ *The peasants were poor.*

❷ *Prices had been going up since 1700.*

❸ *In 1789, the harvest failed.*

Q. ● John has just passed his exam. Suggest TWO long-term, and TWO short-term causes why.

15 Eleven different things caused the people of France to start a Revolution against the King.

France lost a war with England (1756–63).

❺ *The lords.*

6 *The American Revolution (1778–83).*

7 *After 1756, the king was short of money.*

8 *The Church.*

9 *King Louis XVI.*

10 *In 1789, the Estates-General met.*

11 *New ideas about freedom after 1762.*

Tasks

1. Copy the causes onto cards and sort them into two piles – short-term and long-term causes.

2. Put your cards together with another pupil's, spread them face-down on the table, and play a game of 'pairs' with them.

3. Working as a whole class, choose FOUR of the causes and suggest how each cause led to a revolution.

4. Identify TWO long-term and TWO short-term causes of the French Revolution.

Game, set and match ...

Q. Describe a moment that was a turning point in your life. What made it a 'turning point'?

The Estates-General meets

On 5 May 1789, the Estates-General met.

They began with a 3-hour speech about the king's money problems. The Estates-General wanted to change the government, but the king wanted them to give him some money!

The 3rd Estate is Unhappy

There were 3 Estates in the Estates-General – 291 people from the Church (the 1st Estate), 300 lords (the 2nd Estate) and 610 other people (the 3rd Estate). So the 3rd Estate thought they would out-vote the other Estates, 610 to 591.

But then the king told the Estates that they would just have one vote each. That meant that the 1st and 2nd Estates could out-vote the 3rd Estate, two votes to one.

The 3rd Estate were unhappy about this. They complained. At the same time, they asked the people to make lists of things they were unhappy about (see **Source B**, page 4).

A Turning Point in History

Now the king was unhappy. He told the 3rd Estate to keep quiet. Then, on 20 June 1789, when the 3rd Estate went to meet, they found that the king had shut the hall and locked the doors.

The 3rd Estate were angry. They went to an indoor tennis court next door. The king did not know what to do, so he let them. He did not know it, but it was the start of the Revolution.

Q. The king said he ruled by the will of God. What makes **Source A** the start of a revolution?

The king did not try to stop the 3rd Estate meeting; the hall had been shut for some building work.

SOURCE **A**

We sit here by the Will of the People, and we will never leave.

▲ *What the 3rd Estate said to the king, when he told them to leave the Tennis Court.*

SOURCE **B**

What is the 3rd Estate? Everything.
What was it till now? Nothing.
What does it want to be? Something.

▲ *Written by one of the people at the Estates-General, 1789.*

The National Assembly

The king let the 3rd Estate keep on meeting.
The 3rd Estate called itself the National
Assembly.   It said it was the People's
35 government.   It began to try to change things.
   But in the Assembly, everything was in chaos.
People shouted, cheered and clapped.   People
who supported the king took out their swords
and planned to kill the others.   Then in would
40 come a mob and run to the front of the hall,
shouting: 'We are hungry. We have no food.
Down with the lords!'

NEW WORDS

National Assembly,
chaos, shout, cheer,
supported, swords

When the queen
heard that the poor
had no bread, she asked:
'Why do they not
eat cake?'

Tasks

1. Imagine you are a member of the Assembly.   You go home.
Tell your family about everything that has happened and is
happening there.

2. Look back through pages 2–8.   Why was there a revolution in 1789?

SOURCE C

▲ *The Estates-General.   The king sits at the far end, under the crown.   The Church
are on the left, the lords on the right, and the 3rd Estate at the bottom of the picture.*

A picture paints a thousand words

YOUR MISSION: to give a presentation on the painting 'The Tennis Court Oath' by J-L David.

NEW WORDS

oath: promise.

message

The Tennis Court Oath

On 20 June 1789, the 3rd Estate went to the Tennis Court and took an oath never to stop meeting until the government was changed.

5   This is a painting of the Oath by J-L David. But he was not there, and he put in people who became important later!   The painting does not show what happened.   It has a message . . .

The king did nothing on 20 June 1789 because his son had just died.

Tasks

Find in the painting the things listed on the left, and try to guess the message. Then check if you were right by following the strings.

a. Wind blows	France turned upside down
b. Light shines	Everyone is united
c. Hands reaching out	They want change
d. People cheering	Freedom is coming
e. Hand on heart	New ideas
f. Man, Bishop and lord hug	Honesty, goodness
g. Umbrella inside out	Truth will show the way
h. Man writing	Everyone is happy

Now, imagine you are a guide at an art museum. Give a presentation to the class about the painting, as though they were visitors to your art gallery.

◄ *The Tennis Court Oath, by J-L David. Can you see the one man who would not take the Oath?*

The fall of the Bastille, 14 July 1789

Your Mission: to work out what really happened on Bastille Day, 1789.

NEW WORDS

capture

remember

overthrow

rebellion: when people attack the government.

Governor: man in charge of the Bastille.

chains

surrender

Bastille Day

On 14 July 1789, the people of Paris captured a castle in Paris called the Bastille.   Then they knocked it down, stone by stone.

5   When the king was told what had happened, he asked, 'Is this a rebellion?'   He was told, 'No, it is a revolution.'

Every year, on 14 July, the people of France still remember 'Bastille Day' as the time when

10 the king's bad government was overthrown.

But what happened?

What the people said at the time:

1. The Bastille was a big castle, where the king's prisoners were kept in chains.
2. King Louis XVI was bringing soldiers to Paris stop the Revolution.
3. The people attacked the walls.
4. The defenders shot at the people and killed many of them.
5. There was a long battle.
6. They captured the castle.
7. The people killed the Governor.
8. They set the prisoners free.

Tasks

1. Compare what people said at the time (**1–8**) to what historians say today (**a–h**). How are the two accounts different?

2. Why do you think the two accounts are so different?

3. Write a Diary entry for 14 July 1789, starting 'Today has been very exciting . . .'

> The King kept a diary. His entry for 14 July 1789 read: 'Nothing'.

What historians think today:

a. The Bastille was a prison. It only had 7 prisoners – 3 of them were madmen.
b. The food was good.
c. Gunpowder was stored there for guns.
d. The king was bringing soldiers to Paris and people were afraid. Bread prices were high.
e. The people of Paris were angry and attacked the Bastille.
f. The Governor tried hard to stop the battle. He did not fire his cannons. He only had 30 soldiers and 8 old men.
g. The Governor surrendered because he was told that he and his men could go free.
h. The people went in, killed the Governor and cut off his head. They freed the prisoners.

How is the Bastille remembered?

Your Mission: to plan an event to celebrate Bastille Day.

Bastille Day

The people of France still remember Bastille Day. They have street parties all over France.   All the firemen of Paris hold dances.

5   The fall of the Bastille still affects us today!

Q. ● Make a list of things that are wrong in the world.

SOURCE A

There is still a lot to do.   Some of us are free, but we are not equal.

The Bastille shows us that, if we want the world to be a better place, we have to DO something.

▲ *Written by a modern writer.*

SOURCE B

Bastille Day was the time when the people of France took power from the king.

It was the start of our freedom.

▲ *Written by the President of France.*

SOURCE C

▲ *A picture, painted long after 1789, showing the fall of the Bastille.   It shows many more people attacking the Bastille than were there at the time.   Can you think why?*

SOURCE D

The leader of China was asked how the French Revolution had changed the world. He said: 'It is too soon to say'.

◄ *A painting of 1790. It makes the Bastille look much worse than it really was. Can you think why?*

SOURCE E

storm the streets to end hunger

bastille day 1999

▲ *On Bastille Day 1999 there was a fun run to help people in the world who do not have enough to eat. Can you think why?*

Tasks

This is what you are doing for Bastille Day in your town.

1. There is going to be a new statue in the town hall. What will it show?

2. There will be a fun run. What cause will it support?

3. A band will play. Suggest songs they might play.

4. There will be a fancy dress ball. Design a costume for yourself.

5. Write a speech for a famous guest to give at the end of the ball.

IN THIS CHAPTER YOU WILL LEARN:

● How the King was brought to Paris;

● How he tried to escape and was executed;

● TEN reasons the Revolution turned violent.

NEW WORDS

fall, abolish, lose

Declaration: sets out people's ideas.

crowd, chase, guards

The Rights of Man

After the fall of the Bastille, the National Assembly began to change the government.

On 4 August 1789, they abolished the power
5 of the lords and the Church.   At first, the king did nothing.   He said: 'Even if the lords lose some rights, and the Church loses some money, I am still the king.'

Q. ● What did the king mean in lines 6–8? What would *you* have said?

But, on 26 August 1789, the National Assembly
10 agreed a *Declaration of the Rights of Man*.   The idea that French men had *rights* was new!

Now the king began to try to stop the Revolution!

The main ideas of the *Declaration of the Rights of Man*:

1. Men are born and stay free and equal;

2. Power comes from the People;

3. The People make the laws.   The law must be the same for everybody.

4. No man can be put in prison for what he thinks;

5. All men should pay taxes.

SOURCE A

▲ *In August a new National Guard was set up, which took an oath to defend the Revolution.*

Q. ● What rights do *you* have?   Make a 'Declaration of Rights' for teenagers today.

The Women go to Versailles

15 When they heard that the king wanted to stop the Revolution, the people of Paris were angry.

On 5 October 1789, a big crowd of women met in Paris. They took some guns and set off 20 to go to see the king.

The women got to Versailles in the afternoon. The king was scared. He met the women and gave them some food.

Everyone went to bed.

25 But at 6 am next morning, the women attacked the Palace. They shouted: 'We are going to kill the queen and cut off her head'. They killed the guards. They chased the king and queen in their night clothes round the Palace.

30 The women only stopped when the king and queen said they would go to live in Paris. Then the women took them back to Paris.

'The People have won', said one Frenchman.

Tasks

1. Look at the ideas in the *Declaration of the Rights of Man* (*page 16*). Explain in your own words what each one means. Which ones would stop the king ruling as he wanted?

2. Look at the *Declaration of the Rights of Man* again. Who did the National Assembly forget?

3. Explain why the *Declaration of Rights* still affects us, today.

In 1948, the United Nations agreed the *Universal Declaration of Human Rights*. It began: 'All human beings are born free and equal . . .'.

SOURCE B

▲ *The women go to Versailles to see the King.*

Louis XVI

Historians do not think much of Louis XVI. They say he was a good man, but a bad king.

Q ● Look through 'What historians say about Louis XVI'. Find TWELVE things they say about him.

● Was Louis XVI 'a good man'?

● Was Louis XVI 'a bad king'?

The king tries to escape, 20 June 1791

5 The king and queen knew why they were in Paris. 'They want my head', said the queen.

On 20 June 1791, they tried to escape to Germany. The children's teacher pretended to be a rich lady. The king and queen pretended to
10 be her servants. Soldiers were going to meet them and look after them.

At 10.15 pm, they set off in a coach. They were an hour late, but they did not hurry.

The king was happy. He was getting away!
15 But the coach went too slowly. They stopped to get new horses. They stopped to get out of the coach and have a rest.

By the time they had gone 100 miles, they were 3 hours late. The soldiers who had gone
20 to look after them had gone home.

They stopped to change the horses. The king got out and talked to some people. He paid for the horses.

The man who took the money saw the
25 'servant'. Then he looked at the face on the coins. It was the same man! He went to the next village. There, the king and queen were stopped, and taken back to Paris.

All the way back, the people shouted 'They
30 must go! They must go!'

What historians say about Louis XVI:

● Kind but weak.

● Shy and wanting to please.

● Dull and slow.

● Gentle, nice.

● He let others run the government while he went hunting.

● A greedy eater, a good father.

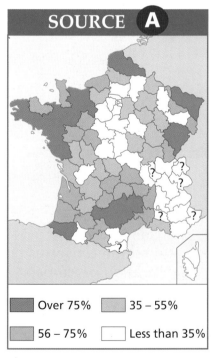

SOURCE A

| Over 75% | 35 – 55% |
| 56 – 75% | Less than 35% |

▲ *Not everyone in France wanted Revolution. This map shows the parts of France which did not.*

The king is executed, 21 January 1793

At 8.30 am on the morning of Tuesday, 21 January 1793, the king got into a coach, which set off for the *Place de la Revolution* in Paris.

35   It took two hours to get there.   All the way it was very quiet.   Nobody said a word.

The coach stopped.   'We are here', said the king, and he got out.   He was not scared. Drummers had been told to make sure he could

40   not be heard.   The king looked at them and they stopped.

'I did not do anything bad!' he shouted. Then they executed him.   It was 10.22 am. A young man took the head and held it up.

45   At first, the people were quiet.   But then they began to cheer: 'Long live the Revolution!'

NEW WORDS
escape
pretend
servant
coach
hour
coin
shy
gentle
drummer
executed
guillotine

SOURCE **B**

▲ *The execution of Louis XVI, showing the guillotine.*

Some people in the crowd tasted the king's blood.   They said it tasted salty!

Tasks

1. Discuss with a partner what these people would have felt about the events of 20 June 1791:

● a poor person who hated the king;

● a lord who hated the Revolution;

● the queen.

2. Now, discuss how they would have felt on 21 January 1793.

The mob turns to murder

Why did the mob turn to murder?

As time went on, the mob – the poor people of Paris – took over the
5 Revolution. They were called the sans-culottes.

In September 1792, they murdered 1,400 lords and priests. They cut off their heads, and pulled
10 out and ate their hearts. What were they thinking to make them do this?

NEW WORDS

sans-culottes

murder, hearts

losing, rebelled

middle class

The poor were called sans-culottes because they wore ordinary trousers, not culottes (knee breeches), which were worn by the rich.

Tasks

You are a sans-culotte. You have been arrested after the September massacres.

Ask your teacher to play the judge.

● First you will be asked: 'Why did you do it?' (Choose the best excuse from **1–10**.)

● Then you will be asked, 'Why did this make you kill all those people.' (Work out what you will say.)

1. We can do what we like now the King has lost his power.

2. The price of bread is high and we are hungry.

3. The King is trying to stop the Revolution.

6. Some lords say they will stop the Revolution.

5. Some parts of France have rebelled against the Revolution.

7. Some lords have run away to other countries.

4. We are losing the war with Austria.   If they win, they will stop the Revolution.

8. The National Assembly is run by middle class people, not by the poor people.

9. The National Assembly is sending the National Guards to attack us.

10. The Revolution has not gone far enough. We want more changes.

The King must die ...

Your Mission: *to prepare a case against the King.*

In December 1792, the king was put on trial for his life. He was taken to the Assembly, and accused of many things. They had not let him wash, and they did not let him take his glasses.
5 He had no coat, only a bit of brown cloth. He looked tired, fat and sad.

In Paris, the newspapers were saying that he had to die. The mob said he had to die. In the end, so did the Assembly. On 17 January 1793,
10 by 361 votes to 360, the Assembly said that the king was guilty, and should be executed.

What would you have said if you had been there?

One of the people who voted that Louis was 'Not Guilty' was murdered that night.

REPORT 1

◄ *The king had tried to escape from the Revolution. He was going to get an army so he could come back and fight against the Revolution – and kill Frenchmen.*

REPORT 2

◄ *There are rumours that the queen is sex mad. This drawing shows the king and queen as a monster. Most drawings of the Queen from this time are not fit to be seen.*

REPORT 3

▲ *There are rumours that the king is a drunk.*

REPORT 4

You are a fat pig.   You cost us 25 million a year.

▲ *Said by a soldier to Louis XVI.*

REPORT 5

The king is 'Mr No' to the Revolution. Why don't we kill him?

▲ *Said by the sans-culottes when they heard that the king was trying to stop some laws they wanted.*

REPORT 6

When the king was just a fool,
'Forgive the fool', we said.
But now he wants to get back rule,
We'll bash him on the head!

▲ *A poem going round Paris.*

Tasks

1. Ask your teacher to be Louis XVI, then put him 'on trial'.

2. First, decide if you will let the king speak to defend himself.

3. Next, working with a partner, work out a speech in which you accuse Louis XVI of treason, and argue that he ought to be executed.   Use all the facts you have learned so far, as well as **Reports 1–7**.

4. Then, taking it in turns, pupils give their speeches.   If you have decided to let the king speak, you must contradict and disprove everything he says.

5. After the trial, take a vote. Should the king be executed?

REPORT 7

He shut the doors to stop the Estates-General meeting in 1789.
He was bringing soldiers to Paris to stop the Revolution in 1789.
He tried to escape in 1791.
He is trying to get back all his power.
He has given money to our enemies.
He has said 'No' to some laws we want.

▲ *What the king was accused of doing.*

4 THE TERROR

IN THIS CHAPTER YOU WILL LEARN:

● **TEN** facts about the Terror;
● **SIX** things the Terror tried to do.

The Revolution has problems

In 1793, the Revolution had THREE problems.

1. The army was losing the war with Austria.

2. Parts of France were rebelling.

5 **3.** In Paris, the people were hungry.

At the same time, some people wanted the Revolution to go further. They were called the Jacobins.

The Law of Suspects

10 On 17 September 1793, a 'Law of Suspects' was passed. It gave the government the right to arrest and execute anybody who was a 'suspect':

Suspects are people who:

● do not love the Revolution enough;
● because of their friends, or because of what they do, say or write, seem to be enemies of freedom or friends of the king;
● have not done their duty to France;
● do not have a job.

▲ *The Law of Suspects, September 1793.*

The Terror

The Law of Suspects gave the government the
15 right to arrest anyone it wanted. In the eleven months from September 1793 to July 1794, it executed 14,000 people and sent half a million more to prison.

a. A butcher was arrested because his prices
20 were too high;

b. A man was executed for giving French soldiers bad wine;

c. All the actors in a play were arrested because the crowd called out 'Long Live the king'
25 during their play.

Other rulers who have used Terror to keep power have been William the Conqueror, Hitler, Stalin and Saddam Hussein.

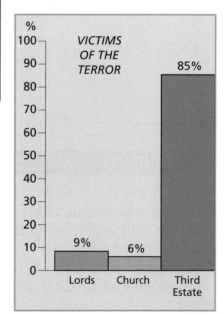

▲ *The Terror did not kill lords and priests. It killed ordinary people – who were not trying hard enough to help the Revolution.*

October 1793: The Queen was executed.

October 1793: Enemies of the Jacobins were executed. Many priests were executed. Many ordinary people were killed.

November 1793: An important Jacobin called Danton said the Terror should stop.

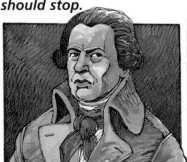

December 1793: 2,000 people were drowned in Nantes.

March 1794: Many important people were executed.

April 1794: Danton was executed.

June 1794: To help the killing go faster, the government said that it did not need to give accused people a trial. Everybody was scared to do or say anything.

July 1794: End of the Terror. 14,000 executed, 3,000 in Paris.

The Story of the Terror

Tasks

1. The arrests and executions were not pointless. On page 24, look at the problems **1–3**, then go through the cases **a–c**. Can you work out which problem each case was trying to solve?

2. Use page 25 to to find: 'Ten facts about the Terror'.

What was the Terror trying to do?

The Terror tried to scare people into helping the Revolution (see **Sources G** and **H**), but it was about more than that.

Some people wanted the Revolution to go
5 further. They wanted to do away with the old ways – and to bring in a new France, where everything would be different. They said that they wanted the People to be free, to be equal, and to be like brothers.

10 Some people said that Terror was an odd way to make this happen: 'Be my brother or I'll kill you!'

What did the Terror try to change?

NEW WORDS

dates

Calendar

months

heroes

forgotten

festival

citizen: a member of the community.

SOURCE A

There must not be any unhappy or poor people.

▲ *Said by a Jacobin. People were arrested if they made too much money.*

SOURCE B

Church towers must be knocked down. They are higher than other buildings, and are not equal.

▲ *Said by a Jacobin.*

SOURCE C

Time opens a new book for History, it needs new dates to write it down.

▲ *A new Calendar was made. The year 1789 was called 'Year I', and the months were given new names.*

SOURCE D

Until our enemies have been chased out of France, all Frenchmen will work for the army. Men will fight, women will make clothes, old men will tell the soldiers to be brave.

▲ *The law of 23 August 1793. The French army grew to 800,000 men, and began to win the war.*

SOURCE E

Roads and buildings were given new names, so that the people of the past would be forgotten, and the heroes of the Revolution would be remembered.

▲ *Written by a modern historian.*

SOURCE F

A big festival to the goddess of Freedom was held yesterday in Paris. Young girls danced.

Then Freedom came in, and everybody sang revolutionary songs and said they would love her for ever.

▲ *The Times, 1794.*

SOURCE G

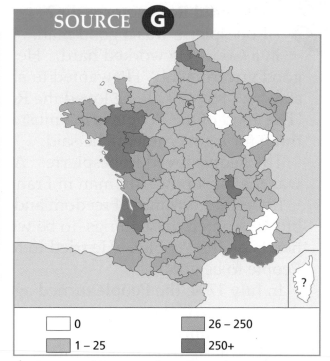

☐ 0	▨ 26 – 250
☐ 1 – 25	■ 250+

▲ *A map of France, showing where most people were executed.*

◄ *The government gave people papers saying that they were good citizens. Everybody else was a 'suspect'.*

SOURCE H

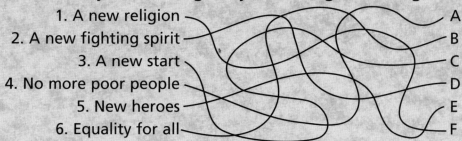

Tasks

1. The list on the left suggests what the Terror was trying to bring about in France. Try to find the Source (**A–F**) which illustrates this aim. Then check if you were right by following the strings

1. A new religion — A
2. A new fighting spirit — B
3. A new start — C
4. No more poor people — D
5. New heroes — E
6. Equality for all — F

2. Now, using these ideas, design a Poster 'A New France', to advertise the things that the Terror tried to do.

Robespierre and the Terror

Why did Robespierre die?

Robespierre was a good man.   He believed in a God.   He worked hard.   He wanted a good government.   He wanted to abolish
5 slavery.   Most of all, he loved the Revolution. 'The good of the People is the most important thing for a government,' he said.

The People loved Robespierre.   After 1793, he was the most powerful man in France.
10 Robespierre wanted Freedom and Equality – but he wanted these things 'to be written on the hearts on the People'.   He tried to force the People to be good.

In July 1794, the People turned against him.
15 An army of 6,000 men came to arrest him.   His friends left him.

Robespierre tried to kill himself with a gun, but he just shot off his jaw.

▲ *A drawing from the time.*

They left him all night.   All next day they made
20 him wait.   There was no trial.   A man put a cloth round his jaw.   Men mocked him, shouted at him; he said not a word.

At 6 pm on 28 July 1794, they executed him. The Terror had come to an end.   Robespierre
25 was dead.

But he was not gone.   Ever since Robespierre, governments have had to remember that 'the good of the People is the most important thing for a government'.

NEW WORDS

slavery
force
jaw
since
joy
crime
Virtue: goodness.

SOURCE **A**

Your death fills me with joy.   Go to hell.

 ▲ *Shouted by a woman at Robespierre.*

SOURCE **B**

It's not enough that he's the boss.   He wants to be God as well!

 ▲ *Shouted by a man about Robespierre.*

SOURCE **C**

Sept 1793	21
Oct 1793	59
Nov 1793	61
Dec 1793	68
Jan 1794	61
Feb 1794	77
Mar 1794	121
Apr 1794	258
May 1794	345
Jun 1794	688

▲ *The number of people executed in Paris, September 1793 to June 1974.*

SOURCE D

The war was won. The rebellions were over. The people had bread. There was no more need for the Terror. But Robespierre said he wanted to kill more people. People had had enough.

▲ *Written by a modern historian.*

SOURCE E

▲ *Robespierre executes the last Frenchman. Everybody else is dead.*

SOURCE F

▲ *Robespierre makes the people play blind man's buff with Death.*

The Sayings of Robespierre

● The Revolution will give its enemies nothing but death.

● Kings and lords are slaves revolting against the ruler of the earth, the People.

● I am the People!

● Children belong to France. They do not need nice clothes, and they will eat vegetables, milk, bread and water.

● We need two things: Virtue and Terror. Virtue without Terror can do nothing.

● There are times in a Revolution when just being alive is a crime.

● The world is full of fools and bad men.

● I am very tired.

Tasks

1. Draw a graph of the figures in **Source C**. What do they show?

2. What is the message of the cartoons in **Sources E** and **F**?

3. Find THREE reasons Robespierre fell from power.

4. Do you like Robespierre? Did he deserve to die?

5 HOW DID PEOPLE'S LIVES CHANGE?

IN THIS CHAPTER YOU WILL LEARN:
- ● THREE things the Revolutionaries wanted;
- ● FOUR facts about Toussaint L'Ouverture.

NEW WORDS

throat

destiny: the meaning of life.

What did the Revolutionaries want?

'The problem with revolutions', said one Frenchman, 'is not getting them started – it is stopping them.'

5   When the Revolution started in 1789, it was led by middle class people who just wanted a better government.   But the Revolution was taken over by the mob, who wanted a better life for the poor.   And the Revolution ended up in
10 the hands of the Jacobins – people who would do anything to make a better world.

It was then (says one historian) that 'the Revolution started to kill its own children'.

In many villages, the poor people broke into the castles of their lords and burned the documents which proved that the lords owned the land.

Q. ● What would you change, if you ruled the world?

DEMAND 1

The job of the National Assembly is to stop every trick by which one man, or a few men, have the right to hurt millions.

It must rule the country for the good of the People.

▲ *Letter to a Young Man, written at the start of the Revolution.*

DEMAND 2

Bread!   Bread!   No more talking.   We'll cut the Queen's pretty throat.

▲ *Said by the women on the way to Versailles in October 1789.*

DEMAND 3

We want to fulfil the destiny of mankind.   Let France be the star of the whole world, and let us see the sunrise of happiness for everyone. I mean Virtue – the love of the country and its laws.

▲ *Said by Robespierre.*

Middle-class people, who wanted a better government.

The Jacobins, who wanted a better world.

The poor, who wanted a better life.

Tasks

1. Match Demands 1–3 on page 30 to the three kinds of Revolutionaries in the diagram on this page.

2. Look back through pages 2–29, and try to find an event that would have pleased each kind of Revolutionary.

3. Find TWO more things that people demanded during the Revolution.

Not your usual Revolutionary ...

Talleyrand

The French Revolution was a time of great changes, but many people lived through them all. One such man was Charles Talleyrand.

5 After Robespierre died, a government called the Directory took over. Then a general called Napoleon came to power.

Talleyrand worked for them all. Then, in 1815, Talleyrand helped to throw out Napoleon 10 and bring back the king; he worked for the kings of France until 1834. One historian has said that his story is 'a history of the times'.

What kind of a man was Talleyrand?

> Talleyrand told off a man
> who drank a glass of brandy in one gulp:
> 'First you should warm the glass in your hands, then
> gently shake it, then smell the brandy.'
> 'And do you drink it then?' asked the man.
> 'No', said Tallyrand. 'You put the glass down
> and talk about it.'

SOURCE **A**

It is not treason if you time it right.

▲ *Said by Talleyrand.*

1779: Talleyrand became a priest, then a bishop.

1785: Talleyrand defended the Church against the King.

1789: The Estates-General. He attacked the Church.

1795: The Directory. He was a government minister.

1799: Talleyrand helped Napoleon take power.

1814: Talleyrand helped Louis XVIII come to power.

Life of Talleyrand

SOURCE B

He was the best minister France has ever had.

He loved France all his life and defended it with all his might.

▲ *Written by a modern historian.*

Talleyrand liked to drink coffee, as long as it was 'black as the devil, hot as hell, pure as an angel, sweet as love'.

SOURCE C

Talleyrand not only outlived his enemies but he plotted the changes that defeated them.

His is the story of a boy born with a clubfoot, a penniless lord who bedded many of the rich women of France, a man who made the wars and revolutions that gave us the modern world.

▲ *Written by a modern writer.*

SOURCE D

▲ *Talleyrand when he was an old man.*

Tasks

1. Using page 32, find FOUR times Talleyrand changed sides.

2. What did Talleyrand mean in **Source A**?

3. Working with a partner, compare Robespierre (pages 28–29) and Talleyrand (pages 32–33):

a. Who was the cleverest?

b. Who most deserves to be called a 'good' man?

c. Who do you like the most?

d. Who did the most for history?

1792: Talleyrand worked for the National Assembly.

1794: The Terror. He ran away to the USA.

1814–1834: Talleyrand was a minister of the king.

1838: Talleyrand died.

What about the women?

Your Mission: to prepare a case that the Revolution betrayed women.

In 1789, the Assembly wrote the *Declaration of the Rights of Man*. Two years later, a French woman called Olympe de Gouges wrote the *Declaration of the Rights of Women*. It began:

5 'Women are born free and equal to men'. She was put in a prison for the insane, even though there was nothing wrong with her.

Then she was executed.

NEW WORDS

insane

trouble

cowards

selfish

SOURCE A

▲ Before the Revolution, women had as bad a time as the men.

SOURCE B

Women are more gentle than men, and better in the home. Like men, they love freedom.

The Revolution believes in equality. But it will not let half the People have a say in making the laws. It has forgotten 12 million women.

▲ Written in 1790 by a French lord who wanted women to have the vote.

SOURCE C

If women have the right to be executed, they should have the right to speak in the National Assembly.

▲ Written by Olympe de Gouges.

SOURCE D

We will carry weapons. We will show men that we are as good as them.

▲ Written in 1792 by a woman called Theroigne de Mericourt. When she became insane, the doctors said it was because she had tried to be like a man.

SOURCE E

The women start the trouble, then the men follow.

They call the men cowards and say that the government will let them die of hunger.

▲ Written in 1795 about the Revolution.

SOURCE F

Man is born selfish. All he lets us do is look after the house.

▲ *Written by a woman in 1789.*

SOURCE G

We want to come home and find the house clean. It makes us angry when we have to wait for them to come home from meetings.

▲ *Said by the men of Paris about women Revolutionaries.*

SOURCE H

Women's life is still 'Work, do as you are told and be quiet'.

▲ *Written by a woman in 1789.*

SOURCE I

We have no bread. If we complain we are arrested. We are not allowed to meet. We are slaves again.

▲ *Said by the women of Paris in 1795.*

SOURCE J

A woman should not have any rights. She belongs to her husband. She only needs to know what he tells her.

▲ *A book written during the Revolution.*

SOURCE K

▲ *A drawing of the women's march to Versailles and back.*

SOURCE L

Women, wake up. Man has become free. But now he will not let his wife be free. Oh, women, women! When will you see?

What have you got out of the Revolution?

▲ *Written by Olympe de Gouges.*

Tasks

Read Sources B–L, then write a letter, or make up a speech, complaining about the French Revolution. You will need to mention:

● What women have done for the Revolution;

● How women have been badly treated;

● Why women deserve to be given the vote.

Women were not given the vote. After 1795, they were not allowed to meet together, or to carry weapons.

What about the slaves?

Your Mission: to design a memorial to Toussaint L'Ouverture.

The *Declaration of the Rights of Man* said that all men were equal. But when the 465,000 black slaves on the island of Haiti asked to become citizens, the Assembly said no.

5 So, in 1791, the slaves of Haiti had their own revolution. The slaves' leader was Toussaint L'Ouverture. In 1794 they won their freedom. It was the most successful slave revolt in history.

In 1802 the French tricked him, captured him,
10 put him in prison and starved him to death. In that year, slavery was brought back into France.

NEW WORDS

island

successful

starved

snake

SOURCE A

A map showing France and Haiti. ▼

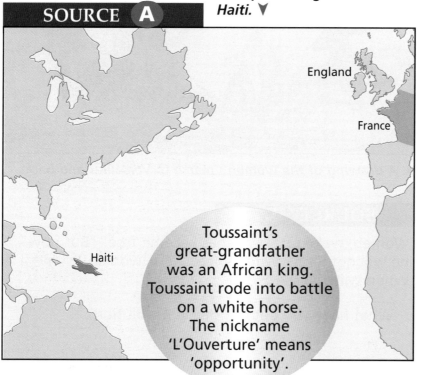

England

France

Haiti

Toussaint's great-grandfather was an African king. Toussaint rode into battle on a white horse. The nickname 'L'Ouverture' means 'opportunity'.

SOURCE B

He was a great man.

He was kind to his friends and a terror to his enemies.

He put God first in his life.

Most of all, he gave his whole life to free black people from slavery, and to make them equal.

There is only one Toussaint L'Ouverture.

▲ *Written in 1853 by an Englishman.*

SOURCE C

France comes to make us slaves. God gave us freedom. France has no right to take it away.

▲ *Said by Toussaint L'Ouverture.*

SOURCE D

I shall not tell you of all I have done for freedom, for the good of Haiti; I love France and the Revolution. I wanted the freedom of my brothers.

▲ *Toussaint always said that he supported France. But when France attacked Haiti, he had to fight back*

SOURCE E

Toussaint is a bad man.   He is a snake who we helped.

▲ *What the French said about Toussaint.*

SOURCE F

TOUSSAINT, the most unhappy man of men!

Though you are dead, you have left behind

Powers that will work for you; air, earth, and sky.

Your friends are joy, pain,

And love which never gives up.

▲ *Written by the English poet William Wordsworth.*

SOURCE G

◄ *In 1803, the French said they wanted to talk to Toussaint, but they captured him.*

SOURCE H

▲ *There is no painting of Toussaint from the time. This was painted 30 years after he died.   Some people think that the artist tried to make him look like a monkey.*

Tasks

1. Why did Wordsworth call Toussaint 'unhappy' (**Source F**)?

2. What did the French think about Toussaint (**Sources E** and **H**)?

3. Make a list of FOUR things that you have learned about Toussaint.

4. Was Toussaint a success or a failure?

5. Design EITHER a monument OR a statue OR a poster as a memorial to Toussaint L'Ouverture.

What about the workers?

Your Mission: to decide if the Revolution improved the lives of the poor.

The Jacobins had promised: 'There must not be any poor people'. Yet in 1795, hungry sans-culottes ran through the streets shouting, 'We want bread!'

5   Did poor people get *anything* from the Revolution?

NEW WORDS

soup

luxury

impossible

level

tyrant: a bad ruler who has all the power.

higher

obey

SOURCE A

Vive le Roi, Vive la Nation.

> Between May and September 1795, the price of sugar went up 6 times, the price of firewood 3 times. In all, the cost of living went up 3000% 1790–5.

◄ *In August 1789, rich people gave up a lot of their land and rights. This picture shows the rich people carrying a poor man, who is saying 'I knew it would be our turn one day'.*

SOURCE B

The lords and the Church never had the same power over the poor. Instead, the government sent an army of police and taxmen. Poor people must have thought the cost of freedom was too high.

▲ *Written by a modern historian.*

SOURCE C

¾ of the people of Paris lives off bread and thin soup. Vegetables are a luxury.

▲ *Written by a Frenchman at the time.*

SOURCE D

Equality is impossible. We need to look after the rich people.

▲ *Written by a member of the government in 1794.*

SOURCE

▲ *On Sunday, 17 July 1792, many poor workers went to complain that the Revolution was only helping the middle classes. The army shot them.*

SOURCE H

In 1789, Louis XVI was a 'tyrant', but his government was weak. By 1799, there were more laws, and the army made people obey them. Taxes and prices were higher. The Revolution gave people 'rights', but it took away their freedom.

▲ *Written by a modern historian.*

SOURCE F

A law of May 1793 fixed the price of food. But it also fixed the level of wages.

The workers hated it.

And in 1794, the government abolished it.

▲ *Written by a modern historian.*

SOURCE G

The rich had the land in 1789, and rich people had the land in 1799.

They were different rich people, but they were still rich.

▲ *Written by a modern historian.*

SOURCE I

The workers were worse off. A law of 1791 stopped workmen getting together to ask for higher wages.

▲ *Written by a modern historian.*

Tasks

It is 1795, and you are organising a protest. Use pages 38–39 to think up possible slogans for the banner you will carry.

6 THE END OF THE REVOLUTION?

IN THIS CHAPTER YOU WILL LEARN:

● FOUR problems facing the Directory;

● SIX good things Napoleon did for France;

● FIVE different fashions during the Revolution.

NEW WORDS

Council
Emperor
Bank of France
Metric system
cartoon
secret
opposition
apply
Nature

After Robespierre

The men who killed Robespierre were middle class, and they wanted power. They set up a new government called the Directory – it had a
5 kind of parliament called the 'Council of 500'.

The men of the Directory had no time for the poor. 'The country must be governed by the best citizens', wrote one of them, 'and the best citizens are those who own land'.

Napoleon described the English as 'a nation of shopkeepers … always eating, always drunk, and no conversation'.

No bread *The mob* *Rebellions* *War*

The Directory faced many problems all at the same time.

10 ## The Directory

The Directory was not a good government. Prices went up. The poor did not have enough to eat. There were rebellions.

For most of the time, the Directory was at war.
15 In this, it was successful. A general called Napoleon won many battles.

But by 1799, people were saying that France needed a king again!

▲ *Napoleon as the English saw him, trying to take over the world.*

Napoleon takes power

20 In 1799, Napoleon came back to Paris.   On 10 November 1799, he sent an army of men to take over power from the Directory, and walked into the Council of 500.

25   They rushed at him, shouting 'Kill, kill'.   It was no use. Napoleon sent in the soldiers and took over the government.   'The Revolution is ended,' he said.

In 1804, Napoleon made himself the Emperor.   He turned out to be a good ruler.   He kept law and order in France.   He made new laws, and set up the Bank of France, new schools and better roads.   He brought in the metric system (metres and litres) which we still use today.

   But, writes one historian, 'Napoleon killed freedom'.

30

35

40

The Sayings of Napoleon

- Power is never foolish.
- The People are blockheads.
- There is one secret to ruling – that is to be strong.
- There is no need for an opposition party.   It just makes the government look bad.
- I am a soldier.
- I am not like other men – laws do not apply to me.
- Nature has made women the slaves of men.
- People who do not believe in God should be shot.
- What was the Revolution?   I was!

SOURCE A

▲ *This English cartoon sees Napoleon as a crocodile, and the Council of 500 as frogs.*

Tasks

1. List SIX good things that Napoleon did for France.

2. Imagine you are one of the people below, and say what 'you' feel about Napoleon taking power:

- a man who took the Tennis Court Oath in 1789;
- a Jacobin.

3. List all the evidence that shows that 'Napoleon killed freedom'.

If the cap fits ...

INVESTIGATION

Fashions de Paris 1789
Before the Revolution.

Fashions de Paris 1790
The start of the Revolution.

Fashions de Paris 1793

During the Terror.

It is a saying that 'clothes make the man'.

People wear clothes to say something about themselves. And it
5 was the same during the French Revolution.

Fashion Designer's Notes
1789:   Show how rich you are.
Use wigs, colour, make-up.
1790:   Dress more simply.   Lots
of red, white and blue.
1793:   Look like a worker.
1795:   Show you are not a sans-
culotte.   Show how rich you are.
Bright colours, low-cut dresses.
1799:   Show that you are rich, but
do not go over the top.   Greek
dresses for women.   Men smart.

Fashions de Paris 1795

After the death of Robespierre.

During the Terror,
people held 'Victim Balls', where
people cut their hair short (like prisoners
about to go to be executed), and wore thin
bands of red silk round their necks
(as though their heads had
been cut off).

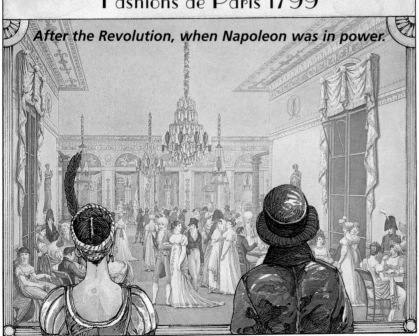

Fashions de Paris 1799

After the Revolution, when Napoleon was in power.

Tasks

1. For each picture, 1789–1799, look at the Fashion Designer's Notes on this page, and explain what the people were trying to say by the clothes they were wearing.

2. Choose one date, and draw and write an article for an imaginary fashion magazine of the time. Start off: 'The latest fashion sweeping Paris is …'.

7 THE FRENCH REVOLUTION

It was a time when Europe was happy,
France standing on the top of golden hours,
And human nature seeming born again.

▲ *Written by William Wordsworth.*

Historians disagree about the French Revolution.

- One said, 'they ended up worse than they started'.
5 - One historian wrote: 'France led the world towards freedom and modern times'.
- Another called it 'a wonderful waste of time'.

10 Did anything good come from the Revolution? Was it all worth it?

Tasks

1. Work in a team of 5. Each member answers one of the questions **a–e** on pages 44–45.

2. Share your findings with each other. Then discuss the question: 'Was the French Revolution worth it – did it achieve anything that made it all worthwhile?'

3. Write 'An Assessment of the French Revolution'. Write SIX paragraphs on:
    a. What caused it.
    b. What it wanted.
    c. How it changed as it went on
    d. Did it change people's lives?
    e. Did any good come out of it?
    f. Was it worth it?

a. Why did a Revolution start in 1789 (see pages 2–8)?

b. What did the Revolutionaries want (see pages 16, 26–27 and 30–31)?

c. What changes happened to the Revolution, 1789–1799? Find out what happened on:
- 5 May 1789 (page 8)
- 14 July 1789 (pages 12–13)
- 21 January 1793 (page 19)
- 23 August 1793 (page 26)
- 17 September 1793 (page 24)
- 10 November 1799 (page 41).

d. How much did the Revolution change people's lives (see chapter 5)?

e. Did any lasting good come out of the Revolution (see pages 14–15)?

Index

Tasks

1. Go through the list of 'People'. Can you remember what they were famous for? Look them up and see if you were right.

2. Go through the index entry 'Events'. Can you remember what happened? Look them up and see if you were right.

3. Use the index to find out:
● Who introduced the *metric system* into France?
● When was the *National Guard* set up?

● The three estates in the *Estates-General*.
● Five different *fashions* during the French revolution.

5. Use the index to find out as much as you can about ONE of these:

The Jacobins, The Terror OR Women in the Revolution

Use what you have found to do a project, with writing and drawings.